FARRAR STRAUS GIROUX — NEW YORK

— CARIBOU —

CHARLES WRIGHT — CARIBOU

FARRAR, STRAUS AND GIROUX
18 West 18th Street, New York 10011

Printed in the United States of America
First edition, 2014

Library of Congress Cataloging-in-Publication Data
Wright, Charles, 1935–
[Poems. Selections]
Caribou / Charles Wright. — First edition.
    pages cm
Includes bibliographical references.
ISBN 978-0-374-11902-7 (hardcover)
I. Title.

PS3573.R52 A6 2014
811'.54—dc23

2013034993

Designed by Quemadura

Farrar, Straus and Giroux books may be purchased for
educational, business, or promotional use. For information
on bulk purchases, please contact the Macmillan Corporate
and Premium Sales Department at 1-800-221-7945,
extension 5442, or write to specialmarkets@macmillan.com.

www.fsgbooks.com
www.twitter.com/fsgbooks
www.facebook.com/fsgbooks

1 3 5 7 9 10 8 6 4 2

— FOR HOLLY, SMB —

Contents

— ECHOES —

ACROSS THE CREEK IS THE

OTHER SIDE OF THE RIVER

No darkness steps out of the woods,
                          no angel appears.
I listen, no word, I look, no thing.
Eternity must be hiding back there, it's done so before.

I can wait, or I can climb,
Like Orpheus, through the slick organs of my body.

I guess I'll wait,
               at least until tomorrow night, or the day after.
And if the darkness does not appear,
                       that's a long time.
And if no angel, it's longer still.

TIME AND THE CENTIPEDES OF NIGHT

Like time, the meadow narrows

                              up to its creek-scraped end.

At sundown, trees light-tipped, mountains half-slipped into
    night.

How easy contentment comes,

Old age at this end, time's double door at the other.

The only way out is the way in.

Now we know which course the drift is,

                              in this drifting dream of life,

As the Chinese liked to say.

                            I like to say it too,

The thunderstorm-floating sky, lightening and lumbering
    gear shifts.

Afterwards, Gainsboroughs to the east and to the south.

How to understand this

Deep sleep,

               deep sleep in the sheared, many-mouth afternoon?

Whatever is written is written

After, not before.

                  Before is blank and pure, and void

Of all our lives depend on.

Prayers rise like smoke, and are answered as smoke is.
Arrange your unutterable alphabet, my man,

                              and hold tight.
It's all you've got, a naming of things, and not so beautiful.

If history is any repeat, which it isn't,
The condition of everything tends toward the condition of
    silence.
When the wind stops, there's silence.
When the waters go down on their knees and touch their heads
To the bottom, there's silence, when the stars appear

                        face down, O Lord, then what a hush.

CAKE WALK

Invisible, inaudible things,
Always something to hanker for,
                            since everything's that's written
Hankers alongside with them,
The great blue heron immobile and neck-torqued on the fence
    post,
A negative pull from the sun-swept upper meadow . . .
Eleven deer in a Mark Morris dance of happiness
Are lighter than light, though heavier
                            if you blink more than once.
There's light, we learn, and there's Light.

To do what you have to do—unrecognized—and for no one.
The language in that is small,
                            sewn just under your skin.
The germs of stars infect us.
The heron pivots, stretches his neck.
He hears what we do not hear,
                           he sees what we're missing.
The deer walk out the last ledge of sunlight, one by one.

WATERFALLS

When is it we come to the realization
                          that all things are wandering away?
Is it age, is it lack of adoration, is it
Regret there's no ladder to the clouds?
Whatever, we inhabit the quotidian, as we must,
While somewhere behind our backs,
                          waterfalls tumble and keep on going
Into the deep desire of distance.

THE CHILDHOOD OF ST. THOMAS

Three-quarters now of waning moon,

                         cold, late summer sky.

Over the broken promises of the day, the nun

Spreads out her wimple and starry cape.

Whose childhood could hold such purity,

                   such fire-blown eyelids of the dead?

It is a wound that cannot be touched.

Even by either hand of St. Thomas.

                       Wish him well.

His supper was not holy, his gesture not sinless.

May ours be equal to his,

              whatever sky we live under.

EVERYTHING PASSES, BUT IS IT TIME?

Sunset same color as maple tree
In my neighbor's yard—
Nature and nature head-butt,
Golden persimmon.
                    And if the stairs to paradise
Are that color, who wouldn't put his old Reeboks down?
Gently, however, O so gently.
The membrane of metaphor is weak,
                              and has no second step.

"Don't play too long, don't play too loud, and don't play the
    melody."
Nature's deaf to this beautiful injunction.
                              And that's okay.
One should live one's life as an acolyte walking into the temple,
Oblivious, the heavens exploding around you,
Your heart conflicted, your footfalls sure.
Time is your enemy,
                    time and its fail-safe disgrace.
Open your arms, boys, take off your shirts.

HOMAGE TO SAMUEL BECKETT

There is a heaviness inside the body
                                that leans down, but does not touch us.
There is a lassitude that licks itself, but brings no relief.
There is a self-destructiveness no memory can repeal.
Such breath in the unstopped ear,
                                such sweet breath, O, along the tongue.

Cloud swatches brilliance the sky
Over the Alleghenies,
                                unpatterned as Heaven.
Across the street, Amoret's family picnic has ended.
Memorial Day,
                                the dead like plastic bags in the blown trees.

In Paradise, springtime never arrives.
                                            The seasons
Are silent, and dumb, and ghost-walk outside our windows.
And so it is down here—
                                we grovel on our extremities
And rise, rise up, halfway to where the new leaves begin.

And thus, unexpectedly, a small rain commences,
Then backs off.
        The sunlight continues its dying fall.
And dying, one hopes to think, will be such a slide, a mild jolt,
Like shifting from formlessness to form.

CRYSTAL DECLENSION

Well, two things are certain—
                              the sun will rise and the sun will set.
Most everything else is up for grabs.
It's back on its way down now
As a mother moose and her twin calves
Step lightly, lightly
                              across the creek through the understory
And half-lit grasses,
Then disappear in a clutch of willow bushes.
                                        If one, anyone,
Could walk through his own life as delicately, as sure,
As she did, all wreckage, all deadfall,
Would stay sunlight, and ring like crystal among the trees.

GRACE II

It's true, the aspirations of youth burn down to char strips with
    the years.
Tonight, only memories are my company and my grace.
How nice if they could outlive us.
                                     But they can't. Or won't.
No Indian summer for us. It's rough and it's growing dark,
The sunset pulling the full moon up by its long fingernails.
It's better this way.
                 The unforgiven are pure, as are the unremembered.

HEAVEN'S EEL

A slight wrinkle on the pond.
Small wind.
            A small wind and the rumpled clouds' reflection.
No hum . . . What's needed is something under the pond's skin,
Something we can't see that controls all the things that we do
    see.
Something long and slithery,
                      something we can't begin to comprehend,
A future we're all engendered for, sharp teeth, Lord, such sharp
    teeth.
Heaven's eel.
            Heaven's eel, long and slick,
Full moon gone, with nothing in its place.

A doe is nibbling away at the long stalks of the natural world
Across the creek.
               It's good to be here.
It's good to be where the world's quiescent, and reminiscent.
No wind blows from the far sky.
Beware of prosperity, friend, and seek affection.
The eel's world is not your world,
                  but will be soon enough.

"I'M GOING TO TAKE A TRIP

IN THAT OLD GOSPEL SHIP"

Did the great ship with the bier of the Hunter Gracchus
Pass by this year? Or is it just late?
Or did it finally find the seam,
                        the crack between this world and the other,
And slip through, sails furled?
And drifts now, as it was meant to drift,
                              on pure, unpestilent waters,
Still circling the globe, and out of its cage forever?
Hard to know, George, hard to know,
Its left-behinds still vibrant,
                    its wake still ripply in the evening sun.

So difficult to belay the myth,
                    so difficult to hold
Hard to the transmutation of narrative and imagination.
The real world has its hands and feet in the other one,
Though its head's here, and its heart is here.
The clouds, as they always do, present us the option:
Dig down, brother, dig down deep,
                        or keep on walking fast.

ANCIENT OF DAYS

There is a kind of sunlight, in early autumn, at sundown,
That raises cloud reflections
Inches above the pond water,
                    that sends us packing into the chill evening
To stand like Turner's blobbed figurines
In a landscape we do not understand,
                                whatever and everything
We know about it.
Unworldly and all ours,
                    it glides like the nineteenth century
Over us, up the near hill
And into the glistening mittens of the same clouds
Now long gone from the world's pond.
                              So long.

This is an old man's poetry,
                    written by someone who's spent his life
Looking for one truth.
Sorry, pal, there isn't one.
Unless, of course, the trees and their blow-down relatives
Are part of it.
              Unless the late-evening armada of clouds
Spanished along the horizon are part of it.

Unless the diminishing pinprick of light

                              stunned in the dark forest

Is part of it.

               Unless, O my, whatever the eye makes out,

And sends, on its rough-road trace,

To the heart, is part of it,

                  then maybe that bright vanishing might be.

NEXT-TO-LAST GASP

Butterflies mass by the hundreds in the dip of the road
                                        beside the creek bridge.
Spiders crabbing across the bleached boards
Of the cabin steps, no-see-ums massing in clouds
                                        outside the window.
Hummingbirds gone, gophers in burrows.
Thistles appear in shaded places,
                        as does the lavender star plant.

Dry end of August. Grasshoppers fly
In bumps and starts and short hops
Toward the brown, long-bladed killing fields of September.
I pooch them along with every step,
Yellow and khaki, diaphanous wings into the future.

Last chapter, last verse—
               everything's brown now in the golden field.
The threshing floor of the past is past.
The Overmountain men of the future
               lie cusped in their little boxes.
The sun backs down, over the ridgeline, at 5 after 7.

The landscape puts on its black mask
               and settles into its sleeplessness.
The fish will transpose it,
               half for themselves, half for the water
Ten thousand miles away, at the end of the darkening stream.
To live a pure life, to live a true life,
               is to live the life of an insect.

All life, as someone might offer,

                                rises out of death

And longs to return to it.

It's in that longing that our days shine out,

                                     and glow forth,

And are our comfort into the dark.

For instance, tonight, in the faint glare of the new moon,

Shadow surrounds us,

The tiny torches of the rhododendron leaf tips

Trouble our eyesight,

                and call us into their hymnal deep underground.

Well, we know those songs by heart.

Sing Along Suzies, we tap out their black notes with our pink
    nails.

We are their chorus and Mass,

And process across the yard.

                      We dip our fingers into the cold font.

SHADOW AND SMOKE

Live your life as though you were already dead,
                              Che Guevara declared.
Okay, let's see how that works.
Not much difference, as far as I can see,
                              the earth the same Paradise
It's always wanted to be,
Heaven as far away as before,
The clouds the same old movable gates since time began.

There is no circle, there is no sentiment to be broken.
There are only the songs of young men,
                              and the songs of old men,
Hoping for something elsewise.
Disabuse them in their ignorance,
Lord,
      tell them the shadows are already gone, the smoke
Already cleared,
              tell them that light is never a metaphor.

ROAD WARRIORS

My traveling clothes light up the noon.
I've been on my way for a long time

                                  back to the past,

That irreconcilable city.
Everyone wants to join me, it seems, and I let them.
Roadside flowers drive me to distraction,

                                       dragonflies

Hover like lapis lazuli, there, just out of reach.

Narrow road, wide road, all of us on it, unhappy,
Unsettled, seven yards short of immortality
And a yard short of *not long to live.*
Better to sit down in the tall grass

                                  and watch the clouds,

To lift our faces up to the sky,
Considering—for most of us—our lives have been one constant
    mistake.

"JUST A CLOSER WALK WITH THEE"

But not too close, man, just not too close.
Between the divine and the divine
                              lies a lavish shadow.
Do we avoid it or stand in it?
Do we gather the darkness around us,
                              or do we let it slide by?
Better to take it into our hearts,
Better to let us have it.
                    Better to let us be what we should be.

Tonight, the sexual energy of the evergreens
                              removes us
From any such attitude.
At least for a momentary intake.
                    And then it's
Back in its natural self,
Between the It and the It.
The fly that won't leave the corpse will end up in the grave.

HISTORY IS A BURNING CHARIOT

It is a good-looking evening, stomped and chained.
The clouds sit like majesties in their blue chairs,
                              as though doing their nails.
The creek, tripartite and unreserved, sniddles along
Under its bald and blown-down bridges.
It is a grace to be a watcher on such a scene.
So balance me with these words—
Have I said them before, I have,
                    have I said them the same way, I have,
Will I say them again, who knows
                        what darkness snips at our hearts.

I've done the full moon, I've done the half moon and the
    quarter moon.
I've even done the Patrick Spens moon
As seen by one of his drowned sailors.
Tonight is the full moon again, and I won't watch it.
These things have a starting place, and they have an ending.
Render the balance, Lord.
                    Send it back up to the beginning.

Water people, water upon water sound, the creek music,
Who doesn't love them?
                              Only the deaf, I guess, or wind people,
Their strings over the desert sands, and the deep canyon blow-
    bys.

Who among us can welcome sorrow,
                                 or the sadness of dirt?
Well, empty yourself of all that, empty yourself of yourself.
There are some things that cannot be spoken of,
                                          or thought about.

"THINGS HAVE ENDS AND BEGINNINGS"

Cloud mountains rise over mountain range.
Silence and quietness,
                sky bright as water, sky bright as lake water.
Grace is the instinct for knowing when to stop. And where.

LITTLE ELEGY FOR AN OLD FRIEND

Well, there you have it,

               everything fine and then the heart goes nuts.

Paddles and CPR, slaps and blows.

Jesus, how did it come to this,

               brain just vacuumed and good to go,

Everyone bending over you, not one you ever knew?

In the light they say you enter,

               was Via Mantovana a part of it?

Or the ground-floor apartment on Via Duomo 6,

In Verona, 1959?

Or was it all Le Crete,

            Asciano and S. Giovanni d'Asso?

Sorrow, come pass me from hand to hand.

Time to reset eternity's clock

To the far side of midnight.

Time to remember the unremembered, and the forgotten.

Time to release them, and give them up.

There is no balm, my man,

             not even in Gilead.

— END PAPERS —

THE LAST WORD

I love to watch the swallows at sundown,
                              swarming after invisible things to eat.
Were we so lucky,
A full gullet, and never having to look at what it is,
Sunshine all over our backs.

There are no words between my fingers
Populating the lost world.
Something, it now seems, has snapped them up
Into its speechlessness,
                              into its thick aphasia.

It's got to be the Unredeemable Bird, come out
From the weight of the unbearable.
It flaps like a torn raincoat,
                              first this side, then that side.
Words are its knot of breath,
                              language is what it lives on.

"I'VE BEEN SITTING HERE THINKING

BACK OVER MY LIFE . . ."

We are all going into a world of dark.
                              And that's okay,
Given the wing-wrung alternative.
It's okay. That's where the secrets are,
The big ones, the ones too tall to tell.
The way in is twisty and torturous,
                              but easy, they say, easy.
The way out, however, is unavailable, and not to be mimed.

Hard to remember that when the full moon
                              offers its efficacy
Downwind through the winter weeds,
Unpeeling its limitless hope.
                              But not, at least for tonight, for us.
Not for us, bystanders back from the river of light.
So file down your fingertips, boys,
                              and pull on your skins.
Incandescence is temporary, we know, but it still shines.

And that's it. My life has been spent
                              trying to leave it.

As though an invisible figure in a Schneeman landscape of
    Tuscany,
I've always wanted to be elsewhere,
Hair on fire, a radiance
Undeniable,
My shoes golden, my heart tucked away
                              back under my shirtsleeve.

Not now, not ever, the world in winter.
                      And this is what comforts us,
Bare trees, bare streets, bare expectations.
Our lives are spent here,
                      our ho-hum and sweet, existential lives,
Stories of cirrus and cumulus.
And why not, this world has been good to us,
                      the sun goes up and the sun
Goes down, the stars release and disappear,
        everything *tutta gloria* wherever we turn our faces.

"WHAT BECOMES OF THE

BROKENHEARTED . . ."

Up where the narrow bodies lie, suffused in sundown,
The children of God are stretched out

under the mountain,
Halfway up which the holy city stands, lights darkened.
Above the city, the nimbus of nowhere nods and retracts.

How is it that everyone seems to want

either one or the other?
Down here birds leap like little chipmunks out of the long
    grasses.
Wind piddles about, and "God knows" is the difficult answer.

The children of Heaven, snug in their tiny pockets,
Asleep, cold,
Under the Purgatorial hill.
Soon they'll awake, and find their allotted track

up to the upside down.

Or not. The gravetree estuaries against the winds of Paradise.

Unutterable names are unpinned from its branches.

                                        A couple
Float down to this pocket, and others float down to that pocket.
Star shadow settles upon them,

                        the starshine so far away.

"MY OLD CLINCH MOUNTAIN HOME"

I keep on hoping a theme will bite me,

and leave its two wounds

In my upper arm and in my heart.

A story line of great destiny,

or fate at least.

It's got to be serious, as my poor flesh is serious.

So, dog, show me your teeth and bite me.

Show me some love.

Such little consequence, our desires.

Better to be the last chronicler of twilight, and its aftermath.

Better to let your hair swing loose, and dust up the earth.

I'd like to be a prophet,

with animals at my heels.

I'd like to have a staff, and issue out water wherever it fell.

Lord, how time does alter us,

it goes without saying.

There is an afterlight that follows us,

and fades as clockticks fade.

Eventually we stand on it puddled under our shoes.

The darkness that huddles there

Is like the dew that settles upon the flowers,

> invisible, cold, and everywhere.

When the wind comes, and the snow repeats us,

> how like our warped lives it is,

Melting objects, disappearing sounds
Like lichen on gnarled rocks.
For we have lived in the wind, and loosened ourselves like ice
  melt.
Nothing can hold us, I've come to know.

> Nothing, I say.

TOADSTOOLS

The toadstools are starting to come up,
                              circular and dry.
Nothing will touch them,
Gophers or chipmunks, wasps or swallows.
They glow in the twilight like rooted will-o'-the-wisps.
Nothing will touch them.
As though little roundabouts from the bunched unburiable,
Powers, dominions,
As though orphans rode herd in the short grass,
                              as though they had heard the call.
They will always be with us,
                              transcenders of the world.
Someone will try to stick his beak into their otherworldly
    styrofoam.
Someone may try to taste a taste of forever.
For some it's a refuge, for some a shady place to fall down.
Grief is a floating barge-boat,
                              who knows where it's going to moor?

DUDE

In my mind's eye I always see
The closed door to eternity.
I think I'll take it,
                    and then I start to think I won't.
As though I had a choice in the matter.
As though the other side of it
                    was something inexorable, something fluxed.
As though the though would never exist.

The dog gets sick. The dog runs away.
You've got your mind on transubstantiation.
                                        The dog
Runs away. The dog gets sick, the son calls to tell you
That he's been fired.
                    You've got your mind on transubstantiation.
The world's a mass of cold spaghetti.
The dog runs away, your mind's still on transubstantiation.

The dog's gone missing, the dog comes back.
The same dog, but a different dog,
                            in different weather.
The droop-bellied dark clouds loom
And suck up their forks of light
                            and the dog goes missing

A second time, and who can blame him?
If he disappears again, your mind's back on transubstantiation.

We live beyond the metaphysician's fingertips.
It's sad, dude, so sad.
There is no metaphor, there is no simile,
                                    and there is no rhetoric
To nudge us to their caress.
The trees remain the trees, God help us.
And memory, for all its warmth,
                        is merely the things we forgot to forget.

That's it. The winds over Punta San Vigilio,
Though welcome, are only winds.
In front of us the door tingles.
                            Behind us, the fingertips tingle.
And here, in the back country,
Junk grass grows down to the creek, the lilacs hang their heads,
And our only world surrounds us like stretched skin,
                            and beats its drum.

SHADOW PLAY

It's 8 p.m., Mountain Daylight Standard Time,
                              whatever that may be.
And the lodgepole pine trees start to flex their shadowy fingers
Across the meadow to the waiting back-lean of their brothers.
It's 10 p.m. in New York, Eastern Daylight Standard Time,
                              whatever that is,
And then the divisional waters,
              the North Atlantic humping toward Greenwich,
Where time's a still point.
                    Or it's not, arbitrary headwater.
The shadows don't care, they keep on inching across the
    meadow,
Unaware they might be going backward,
                              unaware
They might be seeping into themselves.
May the turn of the great star be with them,
                              may it tangle their fingers.

In his suit of lights, the Matador comes forth,
                    Leo crouched in front of him.
Aries is gone, and Leo crouches in front of him.
No matter, the blade is deep
Over Seville and the sere foothills of Andalusia.

Out of the Lion scuttle many ignorant stars.
The Matador lifts his blade.
                              The heavens keep wheeling
Until the poor, stupid lion cubs
Are all that is left.
Time has disappeared the Matador, and rolled him into a truth.
And the Lion as well
                    as he rises into the dark firmament.

—FGL

FORTUNE COOKIE

The stars appear every night in the sky, all is well.
The northwest wind, that rattles the skirts of paradise,
Comes forth from just below them.
They are a river too hard to cross,
                                        it has been said.
But the stars don't care, so snug on their blistering thrones,
Giving the waters a glint here and a non-glint there.
Every so often, however, they fall down,
                                        though all is still well,
Their crowns in a straight blaze to nowhere.

These little lights through the fall-stripped trees
Would like to be stars,
These lingering rhododendron blooms
                                        and white roses
Would like to be stars.
But they are just earth fodder, and programmed for rot and ruin.
The stars are otherwise,
                                        above the wind, below the heavens.
That seems a nice fit to me, not too cold, not too hot,
Time in its peregrinations a stop here and a stop there.

PACK RATS

Up to the upper place to cover the bedstead against the pack rats.
The 10th of August and already they're moving in.
Industrial plastic, waste product from logging companies.
Early winter. It won't work,
                              they'll burrow in and nest,
Leaving their blood-colored urine and interminable excrement
Coming and going.
They'll leave us something shining, or bright,
In return. Bright and shining.

This gray on blue on white on gray on blue
Montana August skyscape
Has nothing to do with politics, or human relations, or people,
    in fact.
It has to do with fictions,
                              and where we place ourselves
Apart from the dread apart.
It has to do with what's unidentifiable,
And where our seat is in it.
It has to do with what the pack rat leaves, what's bright and
    shining.

Surrounded by half-forests and half-lives,
Surrounded by everything we have failed to do,
It is as though kumquats hung from the lodgepole pine trees.
Everything's doubled—
                                        once it arrives and once it fades.
Angels, God bless them, rebound from the meadow, bruised
    gain,
I guess, from our stern world.
Back in the pittering dark of the pine trees,
                                        the rats
Are nosing for silver or gold, or whatever glints or shines.

LIFE LINES

Moon soft-full just over the tips of the white pine trees.
Han Shan could have charactered this,
                                        but I can't seem to.
My brush is too short
To find the right rocks and the bark for eternity.

The past is closing fast and is just about in front of us.
I like the wind at its back.
I like the way its butt twitches and its shoulders shrug.
It thinks I don't know where it's going,
                                        but I do, Jack, I swear I do.

The beautiful evenings of early summer, blue sky
At its end, and green of the arborvitae,
                                        green of the lime trees.
Such a wide membrane
Holding eternity back, stretched tight, holding it back.

FOUR DOG NIGHTS

Sunset and dying light,
                      the robin, dark warrior,
In his green domain.
Beyond West Virginia,
                   the horses are putting their night shoes on,
Ready to break through.
On the stones of the imagination,
                         their sparks are like stars.
This is the stepchild hour,
                   belonging to neither the light nor dark,
The hour of disappearing things.

I've made my tentative statement
                      under the threatening sky,
Honeysuckle in deep distress along the snow-slugged hedgerow.
Eschatology is the underart of the gods,
Patches of bull clover in the high desert landscape,
Installed but never instilled,
The bright, shining mirage our hearts are bedeviled to.
Time, great eraser.

OCTOBER, *MON AMOUR*

The first dead leaves lie like sea urchins
                              browned on the asphalt drive.
It's got to be October,
Slayer of living things, refrigerator of memory.
Next to the wilted lettuce, next to the Simone Weil,
Our lives are shoved in,
                              barely visible, but still unspoiled.

Our history is the history of the City of God.
What's-to-Come is anybody's guess.
Whatever has given you comfort,
Whatever has rested you,
Whatever untwisted your heart
                              is what you will leave behind.

—G S

"L'AMOR CHE MOVE IL SOLE

E L'ALTRE STELLE"

I love walking into the setting sun
                                where nothing is visible but light,
And that not really visible, just a sweet blinding.
Then coming back to the world
Unharmed, but altered slightly,
                as though it were not the same setup anymore.

And it's not. The camp robbers are here,
Doughy and black in the dusk-dead trees.
The great wheel has turned a notch,
                                and I didn't even hear its soft snick.
The mallards parade on the small pond, the older ones, not
    the younguns.

Nothing's as far away as love is,
                                not even the new stars,
Though something is moving them
We hope in our direction, albeit their skin's not on fire.

The child steps out of the dark woods, but is not shining.
Something dies off as my friend.
If I could walk back to that light, I would,

                    but it's buried by now, and gone.

DUCKS

Gasoline smell on my hands, perfume
From the generator's toothless mouth,
Opening swallow from the green hose,
Sweet odor from the actual world.

There's an old Buddhist saying I think I read one time:
Before Enlightenment, chop wood and carry water.
After Enlightenment, chop wood and carry water.
The ducks, who neither carry nor chop,

Understand this, as I never will,
Their little feet propelling them, under the water,
Serene and stabilized,
                        from the far side of the pond
Back to the marsh grasses and cattails.

I watch them every night they're there.
Serenitas. I watch them.
Acceptance of what supports you, acceptance of what's
Above your body,
                    invisible carry and chop,

Dark understory of desire
Where we should live,
                    not in the thrashing, dusk-tipped branches—
Desire is anonymous,
Motoring hard, unswaying in the unseeable.

LULLABY

I've said what I had to say
As melodiously as it was given to me.

I've said what I had to say
As far down as I could go.
                              I've been everywhere

I've wanted to but Jerusalem,
Which doesn't exist, so I guess it's time to depart,

Time to go,
Time to meet those you've never met,
                              time to say goodnight.

Grant us silence, grant us no reply,
Grant us shadows and their cohorts
                              stealth across the sky.

THE CHILDREN OF THE PLAIN

Small they are, and rudderless,
They wander in the hot places
                    and touch their burn marks from time to time.
You've seen them, avoided them,
Watching the birds circle over them,
Their blood full of ashes, city boys lost in the sun.

Their eyelids, it happens, are weighed down by birds, small
    birds
And colorless, who lead them
                    beside the dry waters.
They've become the invisible ones,
Their footprints like tiny monuments
In the ever-erasing sands,
                    the ever-erasing sands.

PLAIN SONG

Where is the crack, the small crack
Where the dead come out
                  and go back in?
Only the dead know that, the speechless and shifting dead.
But it does ooze, half-inch by half-inch,
Under the doorway of dejection,
                  under the brown, arthritic leaves.

The clock strikes, but the hands don't move.
                      The night birds outside
The window are gone away.
The halo around the quarter-moon
Means no good.
Is this the hour of our undoing?
                  If so, we are perfected.

WHATEVER HAPPENED TO AL LEE?

What happened is what happens to all of us: we walked
On the earth, we threw a couple of handfuls of dirt
Into the air, and when it came down it covered us.

"SO LONG, IT'S BEEN

GOOD TO KNOW YOU"

Our generation has come to grief, old dears,
                                as all generations have to.
Outlaw of physics.
Well, hello stranger, put your loving hand in mine,
                                   well, hello stranger,
You know me, but you're no pal of mine.
Coming in the front door, coming in the back,
                                   gonna raise the roof lid
On your daddy's shack.
Speaking in tongues, as we once thought that we were, back
    then.

Train whistle, bat swoop,
                    twilight papier-mâché in the crimped pine trees,
Cloud deck assembling its puzzle pieces together
One by one.
               It goes like that.
So snarked, so soon, the tenderness that lurks inside us
Massages its knuckles and slips on its dark hoodie.
It's like that,
             it's always been like that.
I wish I was a bird in a tree.

Watch where you're walking,
There's always something bigger behind you,
                    and something bigger ahead.
Twisty the way, and twisty the place you're going to.
A rock here, a rock there, wind in the trees,
                    bright shards of green glass
The bat swoops over, listening for food.
It's starting to rain and I got to go home.
                    Be good,
See that my grave is kept clean.

— A P O C R Y P H A —

DETOUR

It seems to be done,
                     the world is not enough with us.
True, the rivers rise to meet us in late spring, the trees,
Conifers mostly, give us their incandescent fingerbones,
And the grasses whelp and propagate,
But it's not enough,
                     somehow it's never enough to please us.
And so we turn to the other side.

But what an absence—Jordan's a hard road to travel.
The love that we detoured into,
                     the love that was promised us,
Soon forgotten, Lord, soon forgotten.
Give us our muddy roads, give us our unrequited, forsaken nights,
Give us our barren landscapes,
Give us our desperation,
                     give us back our disbelief.

DRIFT AWAY

At work in the upper field,
                    hay tops little Buddhas
Calming the meadow and all its attendant tributaries,
Porcupine, Basin Creek, and God's blue hand like a skillet lid
Pressing us down to infinity—
We thought it was up, but it turns out it's down, Jack, down.
Either way we're stuck in the middle,
                              not a bad place to be.

Later, sun like a struck medallion
Over the west edge of things,
                    the distance between the woods and water
Immeasurable, tree shadow on water shadow.
I'm here and not here,
                    above and under it all.
These thoughts begin where words end
Back in the timber, back in the sullen nowhere of everything.

I think I'll take a little time off
And fiddle the underbugs,
Sitting my absence,
                    dusk growing larger and larger.

This is the story of our lives, a short story, a page or a page
    and a half.
Eight days after the summer solstice,
Hard frost this morning,
            my life just past my fingertips, drifting, drifting.

"WELL, ROLL ON, BUDDY,

DON'T YOU ROLL TOO SLOW"

Sun out, sun in, cloud gobbets up high, mist candles down
    below,
Start, and the start of the end of things.
Perhaps. But who knows.
                            Recluse joys are only skin deep.
If my life were a dream, I'd be warmer and happier.
But I'm on a different road,
                            mist and sun, and the dust of this world.
Late dusk by now and no birds, what do you know, no birds.

The old have no hiding place.
If it's going to come, you can't outrun it. Depend
On nothing and keep your joy-bag just out of sight.
Two nights till the full moon, a little soft on the lower left,
A ghostly radiance,
                            almost there and almost not there.
The animals know this and sift away, but we have no clue.

Our lives are in ruins, we think, and they seem to be.
The night will not settle them

Or raise them or cover their spare parts.

                                    Who will discover them

And say what our seasons were?

Who will astound himself one night in the lee of the full moon

In the milky forest, in the scattered and milky forest?

CHINOISERIE II

I have tried to devote myself to simplicity
But it isn't that easy.
I trust myself to nothing, not even the star-sprung night sky.

I wish I were able to live in the constant, and wait out
The end, content to live in the come-and-go of things.
But it's hard, boys, it is hard,

                         a regret and a non-regret.

Li Po was able to detach self from himself, they say, and
Lower and blend his self into the ten thousand things.
Would that detachment were mine, Lord,

                         O would it were mine.

The summer tumbles me into its shadowy depths.
It's dusk again, enveloping dusk,
No lights to light my way, not here nor there

                         where I could forget myself.

CHINOISERIE III

After 77 years, who's not a pitiful sight?
Only the blackbirds know my thoughts,
                              a couple of spots
In the cattails and pond reeds.
The mountains stretch away, the cloud mountains and the green
    mountains.

Such an old song, such old words
As they drift across the creek.
                              Late night lingers, water murmurs.
I've listened to wind-spool all my life.
And now this,
        the slow grind-down of things, the birds settling down for
            the night.

CHINOISERIE IV

All one sees in distance is distance,

       clarity of occurrence
Returning to hold us close.
Under the high grass at forest's edge,

    the voles and mice run back and forth and back.

Their distance is not our distance,

       and what they see there
Is not what we don't see. It's something shapeless and strong
And downright unclarified.

I'd like to say it's something I saw once,
But it's not.

    I'd like to say I wrote a poem once on a stone wall,
But I didn't.

     I'd like to say that it's still there, but it's not.

"REMEMBER ME WHEN THE

CANDLELIGHT IS GLEAMING"

The clouds over Mt. Henry are
                        as fine as the clouds over Taishan,
Or those over Mt. Pisa.

The gravel in the creek's bed does not remark on this.
Larch shadows across the meadow lie down in supplication.

In the small pond, the deer drink, the ducks are cool,
                        and the deep clouds hang still,
Half-moon rising behind my back.

If I had the ink, the paper, the knowledge of magical
   transformation,
I'd make a shorter poem,
                   one of redemption lament.

The mountains of the past berate me,
                 tell me I'm gone and will never be back.
Well, who can listen to them?
            Still, I still see them, stoop-shouldered and shining.

What shadows, and how many rock-washed recalibrators

will name us, or number us in time?

Not a one, Jim, not anybody.

LOST HIGHWAYS

Sunlight is black magic,
                      and transubstantiational even, if
It touches the right thing at the suddenly right time.
Somewhere under the mixed sky is a vacant tranquillity.
A white moth floats into it from out of the pine tree's shadow,
A small light inside a larger light.

Settling ash and disappearing smoke
Is what we're left with in all of this.
                          I find I abide in my idleness,
And react to what I look at and, it happens, nothing else.
I watch the sunsets defuse.
I watch the ravens return to their darkening trees.

SOLO JOE REVISITED

Mortality is our mother,

                    mortality is what we hanker for
When the sun goes down.

           And, boy, let me tell you, the sun goes down.
On Solo Joe Creek, for instance, the ribs of his cabin
Exist still, and the trace of the trail
The horses and mules packed in on,

                    and the mile-long trench
He diverted water to
To sluice down the rock and gravel shards the gold hid in.
Or did not, it seems, did not.

Distance clarifies the water sounds at 2 p.m.
What are we talking about, man, a dollar and a quarter
A year from these splotched waters?

                  There's no horizon here,
Only the treetops and half-clouds chasing each other over the
    blue breaks of the sky.
It's all gone.
I'd like to be sad, and say that every one of these outlines
Slices my heart and my memory.
But I have no memory of this,

           and my heart is as hard as the lost riprap.

DOUBLE-DEALING

Orion, the Pleiades, all red dirt in the end.
The story of our lives,
                    so short, so analogous,
Spreads open, empty, silent,
No matter what clothes we put on.
                              As twilight tightens, air
Fills the air. I'm still here.

It is, after all, about darkness.
Something's creeping my batteries, though,
Something in long, black duds, down there to the left of me.
And here it comes, so anxious, so all-encompassing.
Its flash cards say me.
                    All of its other cards say you.

Almost September and the meadow is still green, green.
The widower birds pipe once, or twice, and then are hush.
Nothing comes and nothing goes.
The doors to the mountains remain shut,
Sky still alert, but no moon rising,

                     grasses alert, but then they're not.

Imagine being a true recluse in straw sandals, wet with the rain,
Never able to settle,

              going night after night.
Hard times, then, hard times.
Better to watch the light come and the light go through the
    window.
Better to hear the thunder turn and then return.

                  Renown is a half-full glass.

CHINOISERIE VI

I'm looking across four or five mountains
                                         gone rust in twilight.
No clouds, no smoke-scrim, just mountains dipped in night's
    foreplay.
There is a clear path beyond the dust.
There is a way to reprieve yourself through the empty and full.
There are waters and waterfalls that go on below us
                                    for thousands of miles.

Contentment comes in little steps, like old age,
                                and poems written with spray paint.
Whims come, whims go, but this one stays here,
An emptiness we all share,
                            what falls away falling away.
It's kind of an afterlife,
Root and branch, thistle and weed,
                        we can't get enough of them, we just can't.

Musician says, beauty is the enemy of expression.
I say, expression is the enemy of beauty.
God says, who gives a damn anyway,
Bons mots, you see, are not art or sublimity.
Go slower, go faster, just get there, you've said your piece. Now
    rest in it.

ANOTHER NIGHT IN THE PURCELLS

Sun-circle-between-mountains,
No double vision into the forest,
                              tamaracks doing a second needle-death,
The old folks at home
Looking into the future.
Light gone, tamarack rust gone,
                    darkness, the last clown, sweeping his soft cape.

The music of the sky is endless
And so I sit still, and then
I can't stand it anymore and get up.
                                        Everything is scarce up here
But distance, and so I look at that.
And keep on moving, and look at it,
                              but it never changes
No matter how hard I look.

Whatever we do see starts and ends out of nowhere,
A place we're familiar with
As we try to look beyond what emendates our lives.
We look for another heaven,
                              we look for another earth.
In the Gulf of Alaska, icebergs dwindle and drip.

TRANSLATIONS FROM A

FORGOTTEN TONGUE

What shall I do with myself?
I'm gone, or I am going,

                let everyone forgive me.
I tried to make a small hole in my life, something to slip through
To the other side.

           If I get there, don't bother me with your comparisons.
Nobody knew I was going,

                nobody knew I was coming back.

Under the push of our footprints,

                  the earth is ready for us.
Who knows how long this will go on?
Stand still, young soldier boy,

             don't move, don't move, young sailor.
Whose night sky is this
With no one under it?

           Whose darkness has closed our eyes?

Notes and Acknowledgments

"Chinoiserie II," "III," "IV," "V," and "VI": These poems are deeply in-
debted to *Mountain Home: The Wilderness Poetry of Ancient China*.
Translated by David Hinton. Washington, D.C.: Counterpoint,
2002.

Du Fu: A Life in Poetry. Translated by David Young. New York: Al-
fred A. Knopf, 2008.

"I've Been Sitting Here Thinking Back Over My Life ...": the line
"Stories of cirrus and cumulus" is from "The End" by Mark Strand,
found in *The Continuous Life*. New York: Alfred A. Knopf, 1992.

"Little Elegy for an Old Friend" is for George Schneeman.

"Plain Song": *Georg Trakl: Poems*. Translated by Stephen Tapscott.
Oberlin, OH: Oberlin College Press, 2011.

"Translations from a Forgotten Tongue": Osip Mandlestam. *Selected
Poems*. Translated by Clarence Brown and W. S. Merwin. New York:
Atheneum, 1973.

Grateful acknowledgment is made to the editors of the following pub-
lications, in which some of these poems first appeared:

Appalachian Heritage

The Chronicle of Higher Education (blog)

The Fiddlehead

Fifth Wednesday Journal

The Kenyon Review

Miramar

The Nameless Hour (exhibition catalogue). Richmond, VA: Anderson Gallery, Virginia Commonwealth University, 2010.

The New Republic

The New Yorker

The New York Review of Books

Northwest Review

Shenandoah

The Southern Poetry Anthology, volume VI: Tennessee. Huntsville, TX: Texas Review Press, Sam Houston State University, 2012.

32 Poems

Valparaiso Poetry Review

The Yale Review